MEN-AT-ARMS SERIES

EDITOR: MARTIN WINDROW
ALBAN BOOK SERVICES

The South Wales Borderers

Text by
CHRISTOPHER WILKINSON-LATHAM

Colour plates by
MICHAEL ROFFE

OSPREY PUBLISHING LIMITED

Published in 1975 by
Osprey Publishing Ltd, 137 Southampton Street,
Reading, Berkshire
© Copyright 1975 Osprey Publishing Ltd

paper edition ISBN 0 85045 209 0
cased edition ISBN 0 85045 231 7

Printed in Great Britain by
Jarrold & Sons Ltd, Norwich

Dering's Regiment

The standing army in England, although dating from the Restoration of Charles II, was not properly established until the reign of William and Mary (1689–94). With the bloodless revolution of 1688, the deposed King James fled across the Channel to the protection of Louis XIV, while William, having been proclaimed King on 13 February 1689, set about enlarging his army for the inevitable war with France.

On 8 March 1689 commissions were issued to fourteen noblemen and landowners who were each to form 'a regiment of Foot . . . for our service'. One of these commissions was sent to Sir Edward Dering of Surrenden, a Kentish baronet of substantial fortune and influence, who immediately set about the task of recruiting. As Lieutenant-Colonel of the new regiment, he appointed his younger brother Daniel who already had some military experience, having bought a grenadier company in Sir William King's Regiment in 1684. The first muster was held on 8 March, the regiment's establishment being thirteen companies each of three sergeants, three corporals, two drummers, and sixty privates, a total of 884 non-commissioned officers and men, with one major, nine captains, nine lieutenants, two ensigns, a chaplain, and a surgeon.

Exact details of the regiment's early uniforms are not known, although it is almost certain that they started off by wearing a blue coat, red becoming the universal colour only with the reign of Queen Anne (1702–14). The officers' uniforms were similar to those of the men but were made of finer material and were ornamented with gold or silver lace, a broad sash, and a gorget.

After being issued with 'such arms as have usually been delivered to other regiments of foot', i.e. muskets and pikes, the regiment was ordered to move from its quarters at Maidstone and Dartford and proceed to the Midlands. In July they were sent to Hoylake to embark for Ireland as part of General Schomberg's army, for the deposed James II had gone to Ireland with a number of French officers and, with the help of Tyrconnell, his viceroy, had raised an army to overrun Ulster, where the Protestants had acknowledged William as King.

On 13 August 1689, Dering's Regiment, along with the rest of the Anglo-Dutch Army, landed on

Edward Dering, Baronet, of Surrenden in Kent, who raised the regiment in the service of King William III. (South Wales Borderers)

John Churchill, 1st Duke of Marlborough, Colonel of the 24th Regiment 1702–4. (South Wales Borderers)

the southern shores of Belfast Lough. Schomberg quickly joined forces with the smaller army of General Kirke, who had already taken Belfast without a shot being fired. After the raising of the Siege of Londonderry (28 July) and the rout at Newton Butler, James's army was in full retreat towards the Boyne, but they had left a small garrison at Carrickfergus. Schomberg immediately besieged the town and it was here that Dering's men would have had their first taste of battle.

The siege, though hampered by the inefficiency of the artillery officers and the poor quality of the guns and ammunition, lasted a week. On its fall, Schomberg, though uncertain of his troops, decided to push on to Dublin. After passing through Newry (5 September), his army ground to a halt at Dundalk (7 September), held up by the shortage of horses and wagons.

For two months the army camped on the damp peaty soil, the weather worsening along with the morale of the ill-fed and ill-clothed troops. The British suffered more than their Dutch comrades-in-arms, who, used to foraging, quickly built themselves huts to replace the leaky issued tents.

With the bad conditions came sickness. Among the earliest casualties was Sir Edward Dering who, stricken by a fever from which he never recovered, died on 17 October 1689. The colonelcy passed to his brother Daniel, at that time a captain in charge of a naval vessel.

Although the situation of his forces was becoming increasingly serious, Schomberg decided to keep his position at all costs. He refused to break camp even when attacked by roaming bands of Catholic irregulars known as 'Rapparees', knowing full well that his troops 'if once disordered would be lost'.

Early in November James's army broke camp and withdrew to winter quarters. General Schomberg immediately followed suit and on 7 November his dispirited soldiers started the long arduous march back to Belfast. More than 1,600 men had died at Dundalk, a further 800 succumbing on the transports taking the sick to England, and 4,000 in quarters.

On becoming colonel, Daniel Dering appointed Samuel Venner as his lieutenant-colonel. Venner, an ambitious soldier who had transferred from the Dutch Army, led many a raiding-party during the winter months, harassing the enemy's supply columns and lines of communication.

In April 1690 a much-needed intake of recruits arrived; they found the regiment's morale pitifully low, for, apart from everything else, only £5,500 of the regiment's £9,600 maintenance since September of the year before had been paid.

The summer of 1690 saw the defeat of James II at the Battle of the Boyne (1 July), followed by his flight to France and the occupation of Dublin along with parts of Leinster and Munster, by King William's victorious army. Unfortunately for Dering's Regiment, they, with one British and two Ulster regiments, were left behind when the army marched on Dublin and so saw nothing of the main campaign. William advanced further into the south but his progress was checked in September at Limerick. With Ulster almost secure, Dering's men had to content themselves with beating off the occasional raid by Rapparees

After William's failure at Limerick the army was sent into winter quarters, Dering's Regiment being scattered between Londonderry, Carlingford, and Carrickfergus.

In June 1691, at the opening of the new campaign, Daniel Dering died and was succeeded as colonel by Samuel Venner who appointed Alexander Ramsey as his lieutenant-colonel. Shortly after his nomination, Ramsey led a reconnaissance towards Sligo, consisting of 100 of Venner's men with 200 mounted troops and 400 militia. Advancing towards the Ballysclara Bridge, four miles from Sligo, they came upon a large force of Irish partisans under the command of Sir Teague O'Regan. Ramsey immediately attacked and with such force that the Irish fled in panic, leaving the bridge open for Schomberg's following army to advance towards Limerick, whose siege was to be the culmination of the Irish campaign.

Venner's Regiment formed part of the army on the Clare side of the Shannon, where the grenadier companies had been withdrawn from their respective regiments to form the main attacking force who would storm the bridgehead into Limerick. When the grenadiers attacked, the rebels broke and fled, streaming back towards the town. The officer on the gate panicked and raised the drawbridge, leaving his retreating comrades to be cut down, captured, or drowned

The attack on the Schellenberg. (South Wales Borderers)

as they tried to swim the Shannon. The fall of Limerick (3 October) marked the end of the campaign for Venner's Regiment. After a brief spell of garrison duty in the captured town they left for England, where they were quartered between Bridgwater and Wells in Somerset.

In May 1692, with the threat of a French invasion of England, Venner's Regiment found itself quartered at Guildford. With the French defeat at Cape Barfleur, however (19 May), the menace disappeared. It was now decided that an English army would invade France, and consequently fourteen battalions, including Venner's and a large artillery train, were assembled at Portsmouth under the command of General Schomberg's younger son. After excessive delays, giving the French ample time to strengthen their defences, the fleet sailed on 26 July, but, after the abortive attempt on St Malo, the plans were cancelled and the fleet returned to St Helen's.

On 27 August the army, which had by now grown considerably, was once again sent across the Channel and succeeded in landing at Ostend where, under the command of General Tollemache, they advanced on Dixmude, which fell on 7 September. With the hopes of capturing Dunkirk fading, Venner's men were relieved of garrison duty and returned to England, where in the spring of 1693 they were ordered 'to embark in our fleet'. The regiment was subsequently split up among the ships of the 'Grand Fleet', which included the *Norfolk* and the *Royal Sovereign*, and served with them for six months, after which they wintered in Portsmouth. In June 1694 Venner's men took part in the attack on Camaret Bay led by Tollemache. At the landing the troops came under a withering crossfire and were forced to withdraw, suffering heavy casualties, including the General, who died on the return voyage to Spithead.

In the winter of 1694, after complaints made against him by his fellow officers, Samuel Venner was forced to vacate the colonelcy, his place being taken by Louis James Le Vasseur, Marquis of Puisar. Under Le Vasseur the regiment saw no real active service, and with the signing of the Peace of Ryswick they were transferred to the Irish Establishment and reduced by two companies, leaving them with 450 N.C.O.s and other ranks and thirty-seven officers. In 1701 Le Vasseur died and the vacancy was filled by William Seymour.

In November 1700 Charles II of Spain died, leaving his dominions in Spain, the Netherlands, and America to Louis XIV's grandson, Philip of Anjou. William immediately ordered the twelve regiments in Ireland to embark for Holland; where French troops had already occupied the Spanish Netherlands. After an augmentation in companies, bringing the total establishment to 883, the regiment sailed from Cork on 24 June 1701, arriving in Holland a fortnight later.

On 12 February 1702 William Seymour was transferred to the Queen's Regiment of Foot (later the 4th or King's Own Regiment) and the vacant colonelcy was taken over by one of England's greatest soldiers, John Churchill, Duke of Marlborough.

On 4 May 1702, with the Treaty of The Hague and the 'Grand Alliance' between England, Austria, and the Netherlands signed (7 September 1701), war was finally declared against France.

Marlborough's Wars

The first two years of the war were frustrating and uneventful for Marlborough and his army, the time being used in building up a base in the United Provinces for an invasion of France, Marlborough meanwhile trying to persuade his allies that the solution to their problems was a head-on confrontation with the enemy. In May 1704 Marlborough undertook his famous march to the Danube, a journey of 400 miles, which his army took only forty days to cover.

After forcing a passage across the Danube by defeating a combined Franco-Bavarian Army at the Heights of Schellenberg, Marlborough joined forces with Prince Eugène of Savoy and formed up his men opposite the enemy-held position at Blenheim, where Marshal Tallard with 20,000 reinforcements held the right of the line, the left

being under the command of Marshal Marsin and the Elector of Bavaria.

At 12.30 p.m. on 13 August Major-General Cutts, the overall commander of the infantry, commenced his attack, the first line comprising General Rowe's Brigade, of which the 24th was part. Rowe's Brigade, 'with undaunted courage and unparalleled intrepidity attacked the village on the muzzles of the enemy'. Undeterred by the heavy fire-power of the French, the 24th and the other battalions moved steadily forward without firing a shot; only when Rowe himself plunged his sword into the defensive palisade did they fire their first volley and, dashing forward, tried to force an entry. Greatly outnumbered by the French, the brigade was forced to retire and in doing so exposed their right flank to the enemy cavalry. Cutts, seeing the danger, sent in the Hessian Brigade who drove off the cavalry and covered the withdrawal.

After the failure of the first attack Cutts sent in a second, comprising the remnants of Rowe's Brigade, the Hessians, and Brigadier-General Ferguson's Brigade. When this attack was also repulsed, Cutts was stopped from sending a third by Marlborough, who gave orders to pin down the enemy in the village.

At 4 p.m. Marlborough launched his great attack. The Allied Army pounded its way through Marshal Tallard's centre and, overwhelming the nine battalions in support, forced the French to beat a hasty retreat. With this great victory Marlborough's reputation was made, to the detriment of the French, whose prestige as the 'Invincible Army' was shattered.

On 25 August 1704 Marlborough was appointed to the colonelcy of the 1st Foot Guards, the vacancy in the regiment being filled by Lieutenant-Colonel William Tatton.

The next two years were relatively uneventful for the regiment. It was not until 12 May 1706 that, in Meredith's Brigade, they formed part of the nineteen battalions and fifteen cavalry squadrons of the huge British force which confronted the French under Marshal Villeroi at Ramillies, where, after stubborn resistance, the French withdrew with heavy losses.

In the winter of 1708 Tatton disposed of his colonelcy to Gilbert Primrose, who, after being

General Sir David Baird, Bart., G.C.B., P.C., Colonel of the 24th Regiment 1807–29. (Parker Gallery)

promoted to brigadier-general on 1 January 1707, had for some time been commanding the home-based battalion of the 1st Foot Guards. No sooner had the appointment been made when a sudden scare of a French invasion of Scotland necessitated the immediate transfer of ten battalions, including Primrose's, for home defence. By the time they arrived in Scotland the French had been beaten off, so without setting foot on dry land the ten battalions rejoined Marlborough's army. A short time after their return the regiment took part in the next major action of the campaign, that of Oudenarde, where the French, after fierce close-quarter fighting, were outflanked by the Allied cavalry and forced to withdraw.

Marlborough's plans to march into France were baulked by his Dutch allies so the Duke reconciled himself to besieging Lille. Five battalions took part in this operation, including Primrose's, who lost sixty-nine killed and 208 wounded before the citadel finally capitulated. After Lille, Marlborough immediately lay siege to Ghent and only when this city fell did he allow his troops to move into winter quarters.

As the Allies and the French were quarrelling over the Treaty of Ryswick and the terms of settlement, the French General Villars assembled an army of 80,000 men behind the skilfully planned and extremely formidable entrenchments which he had constructed in front of Malplaquet. After twelve days of hard fighting (from 31 August to 11 September 1709), the Allies emerged victorious, but with a very heavy casualty list comprising some 20,000 men, almost double that of the French.

The campaign of 1710 opened with Marlborough's laying siege to the last important obstacle between France and the Netherlands, the heavily defended fortress of Douai. Eight battalions, among them Primrose's, took part in the two-month siege. When the stronghold finally surrendered the regiment had lost thirty-six men killed and 157 wounded.

In December 1711, after outwitting General Villars and outflanking his *ne plus ultra* line, Marlborough was recalled, for in England the Whigs had lost the election and the Tories, with the backing of Queen Anne, had decided to put an end to the war.

Primrose's Regiment left the Netherlands on 24 June 1713 and sailed for their new station in Ireland. It was 168 years later, in 1882, that the regiment received its reward for the War of the Spanish Succession, when the battle honours 'Blenheim', 'Ramillies', 'Oudenarde', and 'Malplaquet' were emblazoned on its colours.

18th Century Campaigns

Apart from two short sojourns in England the regiment served on the Irish Establishment for some twenty-five years, years that were very dull after what they had experienced on the Continent. In 1717 Gilbert Primrose died and was succeeded by Thomas Howard who was to be their colonel for the next twenty years. It was during this time that the regiment received the sobriquet, 'Howard's Greens', which indicates that the regiment had by this time adopted green facings to their uniforms.

In 1719 the regiment left the tedium of Irish garrison duty and embarked as part of the force of 9,000 men, under the command of Lord Cobham, who were to make a descent on the Spanish coast. After receiving a warning that Corunna, the expedition's original objective, was well prepared for an attack Cobham changed course and headed for Vigo where the Spaniards had stored most of the equipment necessary for an invasion of Scotland. On the evening of 29 September Cobham landed his grenadier companies three miles from the town, where, except for a few armed peasants, no opposition was encountered, allowing the disembarkation of the rest of the troops and stores to be completed without incident.

The next day the British advanced on the town. Seeing the mass of troops coming towards them, the Spaniards spiked their guns and took refuge in the fortified citadel, where they managed to hold out until 10 October, when, after heavy bombardment by mortars and siege guns, the garrison finally surrendered.

Realizing that he had no hope of taking the heavily fortified ports of Corunna and Ferrol, Cobham embarked his men with the best of the Spanish guns and stores and, after destroying what remained, sailed for home, having done 'a world of mischief' at a cost of only 300 casualties.

Howard's Regiment returned to Ireland where

they continued garrison duties until the spring of 1740, when, under the command of Thomas Wentworth, who succeeded Howard in 1737, they assembled on the Isle of Wight as part of Lord Cathcart's force who were to attack the seat of the Spanish Captain-General in the Indies, San Juan de Cartagena. Although the campaign started off moderately well for the British, it ended disastrously. The deadly climate and thick vegetation all pointed to speed on the attackers' part, but unfortunately Wentworth, who had taken over command of the invasion force after the death of Cathcart, was too cautious and delayed the final attack on Fort St Lazar which commanded the town. When the assault failed, Wentworth, all his confidence evaporated, abandoned the venture and sailed for Jamaica on 26 April 1741. In this short campaign the regiment lost ten officers and 781 rank and file. The regiment stayed in the West Indies for another year during which abortive attempts were made on Cuba and Panama. They then returned to England.

In June 1745 Thomas Wentworth relinquished his colonelcy and was succeeded by Daniel Houghton, a veteran who had first held a commission in 1708 and in 1741 had raised a foot regiment, later to become the 1st Battalion Sherwood Foresters. In March 1746 the regiment was ordered to Scotland where they stayed for four years helping in mopping-up operations after the Jacobite Rebellion and later in building roads to open up the Highlands. During this period Houghton died and was succeeded by William Kerr, Earl of Ancram, who transferred to the 11th Light Dragoons in February 1752, the vacant colonelcy going to the Hon. Edward Cornwallis. Shortly before this, in July 1751, a royal warrant had been issued regulating the clothing for the army. This warrant fixed the regiment's facings as 'willow' green and the lace white with one green stripe and one red stripe. It is interesting to note that numbers were now coming into more general use; after 1753 young officers found themselves gazetted to 'The 24th. (Cornwallis's) Regiment of Foot'.

In 1756 the friction between the French settlers in Canada and the English colonists in North America came to a head. The French, while threatening to invade England from Brest,

Officer's (Major's) epaulettes, 1812–16. (National Army Museum)

Officer's coatee of the 24th (1812–16). The lapels have been buttoned back to reveal the green facings and silver lace button loops in pairs. (National Army Museum)

were secretly concentrating all their forces at Toulon, where they were preparing a descent on the Balearic island of Minorca. The garrison consisted of four battalions, including the 24th, all under the command of General Blakeney.

On 18 April 1756 the Duc de Richelieu with an army of 15,000 men landed on the western end of the island. Blakeney immediately pulled his small force back into Fort St Philip on the eastern end, south of the entrance to Port Mahon. The fortress, with its four bastions and underground galleries,

gave the defenders the possibility of all-round fire and good cover from the enemy bombardments. So effective was the defence that by 8 May the French had succeeded in bringing only two siege batteries into action.

On 19 May the tiny garrison's spirits rose high when they saw a British naval squadron under the command of Admiral Byng approaching from the south-east. The next day Byng fought an inconclusive action with the French squadron and, after judging it impossible to help Fort St Philip,

Ensign Pennycuick defending the body of his father at Chilianwala, 13 January 1849. (National Army Museum)

sailed back to Gibraltar where he was subsequently tried by court martial and shot.

During the next month the defenders continued their stubborn resistance, despite the heavy bombardments being handed out by the French. On 27 June, after they managed to bring over eighty guns and twenty mortars into action, the French opened up an unprecedented barrage as a prelude to the final assault. When the attack came the garrison was too weak to hold out. First one redoubt fell, then another; the enemy then managing to break into the subterranean passages, rendering a counter-attack almost impossible. Blakeney, feeling that any further resistance would mean the slaughter of his whole garrison, decided to capitulate.

Richelieu's terms were most generous. He allowed his prisoners the full honours of war, to march out with 'firelocks on their shoulders, drums beating, colours flying, twenty cartridges

for each man'. They were then embarked on French transports which set sail for Gibraltar. It was in November 1756 that the 24th finally reached England, where they received an enthusiastic welcome. The casualties were low, three officers and 123 men killed or died of wounds and five officers and 301 men wounded. Of these figures the 24th had lost eleven killed or died of wounds and two officers and fifty-two men wounded.

On 24 August 1756, while the regiment was still at Gibraltar, they, along with fourteen others, received orders to raise a second battalion, which was done, mainly from the county of Lincolnshire. Thence they joined the 1st Battalion, who, in May 1757, were stationed in Leicestershire. This second battalion existed for two brief years before becoming the 69th Regiment (later the 2nd battalion, Welch Regiment).

The quarrel between France and England had worsened into an imperial struggle between the Prussian King, Frederick the Great on the one hand and Maria Theresa of Austria, strongly sustained by Louis XV of France, on the other, thereby constituting a direct threat to the Electorate of Hanover, part of George II's British dominions.

For three years the British Government under Pitt refused to send troops into Germany where two French armies were co-operating with the Austrians. Instead he preferred to employ them with the Royal Navy in making raids on the French coast, but without much success. The 24th took part in those of Rochefort, St Malo, Cherbourg, and St Cast. Eventually, in 1760, Pitt was forced to send British troops to Germany for the protection of Hanover. Six battalions, including the 24th, embarked for the Continent and for the next three years formed part of the Allied Army under Ferdinand of Brunswick, filling a prominent role in the victories of Corbach, Warburg, Clostercamp, and Vellinghausen.

Although originally undertaken for the defence of Hanover, the campaign resulted, under the terms of the Peace of Paris (1763), in the withdrawal of all French troops and ships from Canada, leaving Britain in control of the whole of North America.

The close of the campaign found the 24th 20

nen short, having only 490 effectives, with 123
sick. After wintering in Münster and Paderborn
the regiment was placed under orders for Gibraltar
where they stayed for a few years before moving
to Ireland.

A few years earlier, in 1770, due to the success-
ful skirmishing of light troops in the Westphalian
campaign, the regiment was authorized to form
a 'Light Company'. This new formation took the
left of the line and, like the Grenadier Company,
who took the right of the line, had two lieutenants
and no ensign.

In January 1776, after holding the colonelcy for
twenty-four years, Cornwallis died and was replaced by William Taylor, formerly a lieutenant-
colonel in the 9th Regiment (later the Royal
Norfolk Regiment).

America 1776-1777

With the French expelled from North America,
the thirteen New England Colonies found themselves in a position where they no longer had to
rely on Britain for protection and, when the home
Government decided to pay off some of the £140
million National Debt, caused by Pitt's irrational
spending during the Seven Years War, by taxing
the colonists, they openly rebelled.

In 1776, three years after the famous Boston
Tea Party, two expeditions were sent from England
to help quell the rebellion. The main force under
Sir William Howe was directed against New York,
where he would await the arrival of the second
force, who would join him after relieving Quebec,
which had been besieged by an American army
under Benedict Arnold since the autumn of 1775.

By the time the 24th Regiment arrived in June,
Quebec had been relieved and the Americans
were in full retreat towards the border. Sir Guy
Carlton, Governor of Canada and Commander-
in-Chief, decided to use his newly arrived force
without delay, reorganizing them into three
brigades and an 'Advanced Corps'. This latter
formation was led by Lieutenant-Colonel Simon
Fraser of the 24th, the command of the battalion
devolving on Major Grant.

Officers' mess plate of the 24th Regiment. (National Army Museum)

After some preliminary skirmishing, in which
the 24th isolated and captured 300 Americans,
the main force continued up the St Lawrence
River and arrived at Sorel whence the majority of
the troops, including the 24th, turned up the
Richelieu River. By October Fraser had pushed
on to Crown Point, only twelve miles from
Ticonderoga, but with a hard Canadian winter
drawing in it was decided to make winter quarters,
the entire force withdrawing to the northern end
of Lake Champlain.

In 1777 General Burgoyne took over the command and in June advanced his army towards
Ticonderoga, a strongly fortified position held by
some 3,000 men. Fraser and his advanced corps,
by making a rapid march through the woods and
crossing the rapids between Lake George and
Lake Champlain, secured Sugar Loaf Hill which
commanded the rear of the settlement. To the
surprise of the enemy the British managed to get

some artillery to the top of the hill which put Ticonderoga at Burgoyne's mercy. On the night of 5–6 July the Americans evacuated the stronghold, leaving behind some eighty guns and a large quantity of stores.

For the next two months the advance continued, Fraser and his corps always leading the way. By 17 September they had reached Stillwater, where 10,000 Americans under the command of General Gates were strongly entrenched on the Bemis Heights, which rose some 200 feet above the Hudson River. On 19 September Burgoyne attacked, Fraser's Corps advancing through some woodland on the right flank. After some heavy fighting Burgoyne's men consolidated their position round Freeman's Farm, only a few hundred yards from the enemy and overlooking Mill Creek, a deep ravine situated in front of the

Officer's 'Albert'-pattern shako, 1844–55. Note that the ball tuft-holder is missing. (National Army Museum)

heights. Here they waited a fortnight unable to attack the Americans who were strong on the left and unassailable on the right and in the centre. On 7 October as the expected assistance from General Howe had not materialized and the rebels were receiving reinforcements daily, Burgoyne moved out in a desperate attempt to find a weak spot on the left flank which might enable him to pave the way for an unmolested retreat. Seeing this movement, Gates attacked and forced Burgoyne back. Fraser, who had been detailed to cover the retirement, saw the centre giving way and quickly ordered his men across to help. This action enabled the majority of the force to withdraw, but unfortunately Fraser was wounded by a sniper and died the same night.

Burgoyne, realizing that his position was untenable, decided to retreat to Fort Edward, a distance of some twenty miles. On the evening of 8 October with the remnants of Fraser's Corps acting as rearguard, the battle-weary soldiers moved off. Delayed by the pouring rain and enemy snipers, the force was soon overtaken by the Americans, who succeeded in getting between them and Fort Edward. General Gates demanded an unconditional surrender but changed his terms when it became clear that Burgoyne would not accept. The British were allowed to travel to Boston and embark for England on the condition that they would not serve in America again during the war.

The campaign dragged on for another three years until 1781, when General Cornwallis was defeated at Yorktown and the Americans finally achieved their independence.

On 31 August 1782 a royal warrant was issued conferring county titles on all regiments not already having a special designation, such as 'The Queen's' or 'The King's Own', in addition to their numbers. The 24th became the 2nd Warwickshires, a title they retained until the Cardwell Army Reforms of 1881 when they became the South Wales Borderers.

After short tours of duty in Scotland and Ireland the regiment embarked for Canada where they stayed for eleven years before returning to England in October 1800, by which time the war with France had taken a turn for the worse.

The Napoleonic Wars

n August 1798 Napoleon's plans to overrun the Middle East and march to India were shattered when his fleet was destroyed by Nelson at the Battle of the Nile. His lines of communication gone, Napoleon deserted his army and returned to France. In March 1801 the British Government, determined to destroy the French Army in Egypt, dispatched an expeditionary force under the command of General Abercromby. It was this force that the 24th and four other battalions were sent to reinforce in June, by which time the majority of the French had capitulated, leaving only a small force under General Menou isolated in Alexandria.

On 21 August General Coote led a force, which included the 24th (part of Finch's Brigade), and captured Fort Marabout, whence he advanced, causing the French to make a hasty withdrawal to Alexandria. This success brought Coote within long range of the city. Siege guns were brought up and on 26 August the batteries opened up with such ferocity that by evening Menou was forced to negotiate terms, which resulted in his men following their comrades back to France.

On 1 November the regiment moved to Malta, where it stayed for a few months before returning to England in March 1802. At the close of the campaign the 24th, together with the other regiments engaged, were awarded the Sphinx superscribed 'Egypt' which was ordered to be borne on the colours.

In 1804 the British Government under Pitt decided to strengthen the army as a safety measure against the gathering invasion force of Napoleon. This increase resulted in many regiments, among them the 24th, forming a second battalion. It was raised at Warwick in September for home service only, but later, after the defeat of the Franco-Spanish fleet at Trafalgar which removed the threat of invasion, the battalion became available for active service abroad.

Meanwhile in August 1805 the 1/24th embarked for South Africa as part of an expeditionary force led by Sir David Baird, to retake Cape Town which was in the hands of Napoleon's allies, the Dutch. Landing at Leopard's Bay on 6 January 1806, Baird immediately pushed on to Cape Town some sixteen miles to the south, where he secured Blaauberg Ridge before the Dutch, under General Janssens, could take advantage of its high position. After some hard fighting, in which the 1/24th bore the brunt on the British right, the Dutch force retired in confusion, leaving the defence of the city to a force of French sailors and Waldeck mercenaries. On 10 January 1807 the British finally occupied Cape Town and eight days later the Dutch troops surrendered.

With the Cape secured and British interests in the East safe, the 1/24th remained on garrison duty for the next four years and was unable to join the 2nd Battalion, now free to serve abroad, in the forthcoming Peninsular campaign.

In 1808 the Spaniards rose against the French after Napoleon had decided to place his brother Joseph on the Spanish throne. Britain, who saw an opportunity to strike a blow against Napoleon, dispatched an army under the command of Sir Arthur Wellesley. The 2/24th was not included in this first expedition, although Sir David Baird, who had become Colonel of the 24th in 1807, accompanied Sir John Moore's abortive advance on Madrid and the heroic retreat to Corunna. In April 1809 Wellesley returned to Portugal with a mixed force of British, Portuguese and Spanish troops, the 2/24th being one of the twenty British battalions.

By 22 July Wellesley's main force had advanced to the outskirts of the village of Talavera. Six days later Marshal Junot's French Army, outnumbering the British two to one, attacked the Allied positions. This battle proved to be one of the most difficult of the war, costing Wellesley some 5,000 men while the French lost over 7,000. The 2/24th had one officer and seventy men killed and ten officers and 268 men wounded, almost fifty per cent of their initial strength. Talavera ranks as one of the greatest days in the regiment's history and was the first of nine battle honours that they won during the Peninsular War. On 26 August Sir Arthur Wellesley was raised to the

Group of officers, N.C.O.s and men, 1862. Note the sergeant-major's ranking (left) and the bandsman and band-boy (right) in white tunics with green collars and slashed cuff-flaps. (South Wales Borderers)

peerage and adopted the title of Viscount Wellington of Talavera.

After Wellington's victories over Marshal Masséna at Busaco in September 1810 and at Fuentes de Onoro in May 1811, the British besieged Cuidad Rodrigo. Unfortunately the 2/24th did not receive this battle honour, for although their part in the siege was equal to that of the other battalions who did receive the honour, they did not participate in the storming of the citadel.

The regiment's next action came at Salamanca on 22 July 1812, where, after a violent forty-minute encounter, the broken French Army retreated. Three months later the battalion found itself at Burgos where they were chosen by Wellington to force the breach. This they did with a spirited attack, pressing home so quickly that

the French fell back, leaving the way clear for the backing-up force to move in. The battalion' casualties were comparatively low: twelve mer were killed and two officers and fifty-six mer wounded.

During the remainder of the campaign the regiment, now veterans, marched across Spain slowly pushing the French towards their own border. After their defeat at Vittoria, the French withdrew across the Pyrenees where, hampered by the bitter weather and increasing sickness, they were defeated at the battles of Nivelle and Orthes On 6 April 1814 Napoleon's abdication finally brought the Peninsular campaign to an end. On 24 November 1814 the 2nd Battalion was disbanded, the remaining 300 men forming a depot and training cadre for the 1st Battalion.

India

On 10 June 1810 the 1st Battalion, its tour of duty in South Africa at an end, embarked on five troop transports at Cape Town and sailed for India, but two of the ships put back into port, leaving the rest to continue their journey. Off the island of Madagascar the small convoy was attacked by French warships and two, carrying headquarters and four companies, were captured, but not before Colonel Marriot had the colours and regimental records thrown overboard. The other East Indiaman, though badly damaged, succeeded in escaping during the night. The prisoners were taken to the French-held island of Mauritius where they remained until it was captured by the British five months later. In March 1811 Colonel Marriot's party rejoined the rest of the battalion at Calcutta.

The long-standing troubles with the Kingdom of Nepal came to a head in 1814 and caused the 1/24th to be moved to Dinapur in the north. In November they joined the eastern column of General Marley's army bound for the Gurkha capital, Katmandu. After a very hard and difficult two-year campaign in the Himalayan foothills, peace was finally signed on 6 March 1816 and the 1/24th returned to Dinapur.

Immediately upon their return the flank companies were sent to Allahabad, where they formed part of the punitive expedition being sent against the Pindaris and their Maratha supporters. In March 1818 they returned to Dinapur. After the Pindari War the regiment remained in India for another five years, moving from garrison to garrison before they prepared to embark for home, landing in England in July 1823.

Between 1825 and 1841 the regiment served four years in Ireland and then moved to Canada, where they helped suppress the 1838 rebellion before returning home.

September 1846 found the regiment once again stationed in India. The First Sikh War (1845–6) had left the Sikh power unbroken and its leaders incensed at the British demands. In 1848 the murder of two British officers at Multan

sparked off new hostilities in which the regiment was to play a tragic but glorious role.

At the beginning of November the regiment joined Sir Hugh Gough's Army of the Punjab at Ferozepore, where they were brigaded with the 25th and 45th Bengal Native Infantry in the 2nd Division. On 8 November Gough crossed the River Sutlej, determined to bring the Sikh leader, Shere Singh, to battle, and by 13 January 1849 he had occupied the village of Chilianwala. Not expecting an attack, arms were piled, guns parked, and horses off-saddled. Lieutenant Macpherson of the 24th, having finished his duties, climbed a tree and looked out over the broken ground and jungle in front of him. To his surprise he saw 'something flitting to and fro' which he immediately recognized as the turbans of the enemy. Jumping down from the tree, Macpherson raised the alarm just as the Sikhs opened up with heavy and accurate artillery fire. The British were caught completely by surprise. Buglers sounded 'Stand to' and the troops grabbed their muskets and formed up.

The 2nd Division, now under the command of Colin Campbell, was on the left, having Pennycuick's Brigade (H.M.'s 24th Regt, 25th and 45th N.I.) on its right. Just before Campbell moved off to direct the movements of Hogan's Brigade on the left, he told Pennycuick and the 24th that there was to be no firing; the work was to be done with the bayonet. This order was later described by Gough as 'an act of madness'.

At 3 p.m. the advance started, the 24th in the centre with their grenadier company skirmishing ahead. After covering some 200 yards they entered the thick jungle well within range of the enemy guns, which opened fire with devastating effect. Although no order to charge was given, the pace increased, so much so that the 24th were well ahead of the sepoys on their flanks. The grenadier company were the first to reach the guns, only to be forced back, but as the rest of the regiment came up they surged forward again and, though the Sikhs fought bravely, they failed to save the cannon, which were spiked by a small party under Lieutenant Lutman. The colour party was wiped out within a few yards of the guns and the centre company of the 24th was almost annihilated by repeated counter-attacks; but the remnants stood their ground. Inside the enemy positions Colonel

Assistant-Surgeon Douglas, V.C. This officer and four privates, Bell and Murphy among them, were awarded the Victoria Cross for their action at the Andaman Islands in May 1867. These were the first members of the regiment to be awarded the Victoria Cross. (South Wales Borderers)

Private Bell, V.C. (South Wales Borderers)   Private Murphy, V.C. (South Wales Borderers)

Pennycuick fell mortally wounded, and his son, newly joined from Sandhurst, was shot as he reached his father's side.

The heavy casualties in the centre had weakened the line so much that the Sikhs managed to break through and, as no support came from the Native Infantry, the regiment was forced back through the jungle, sustaining heavy losses as they retreated. As soon as they reached the far side of the jungle, Captain Blachford, almost the only captain unhurt, rallied the men and re-formed the ranks for a counter-attack. This action, though disastrous for the regiment, enabled Hogan's Brigade, on the left, to advance and attack the Sikh line from the flank, forcing the enemy to retire.

By the evening torrential rain was pouring down on the wounded, many of them lying in the wet jungle without food or drink, waiting to be found by one of the search parties. Of the thirty-one officers and 1,065 other ranks belonging to the 24th who had gone into action, thirteen officers and 225 men had been killed and nine officers and 278 men wounded. The Queen's colour was lost, one account stating that it may have been buried with Private Connolly who had wrapped it round his body in order to save it and had then been killed. The regimental colour was safely brought in by Private Perry who rescued it when Ensign Collis was killed.

On 21 February 1849 the two armies met once again at Gujerat. After bombarding the Sikh batteries for three hours, the British made a concerted attack, forcing the rebels to retreat. After Shere Singh's surrender at Rawalpindi (14 March 1849) the regiment was stationed at Waziribad before moving on to Sialkot in 1852. In March 1853 three more battle honours were added to the regiment's list, those of 'Punjab', 'Chilianwala', and 'Gujerat'.

In May 1857 the regiment was at Rawalpindi when the Mutiny broke and, although only on the fringe of the affected area, had its share of the action, notably at Jhelum, where 300 men of the 1st Battalion with three pieces of light artillery successfully attacked and drove off 1,000 well-armed mutineers.

In March 1861, after 'fifteen years of memorable services in India', the battalion embarked for home.

In the next ten years they moved from England to Ireland, then on to Malta and Gibraltar before finally being sent to South Africa in November 1874.

A new 2nd Battalion, the third in the regiment's history, was raised at Sheffield on 3 June 1858. After a short spell of recruiting and the presentation of colours by Lady Wharncliffe on 3 May 1859, the thirty-two officers and 779 N.C.O.s and men moved to the new military camp at Aldershot. Their stay at Aldershot was a short one, for an unfortunate incident with some men from a militia battalion resulted in a personal telling-off from the Duke of Cambridge and a tour of duty on the island of Mauritius.

After a pleasant sojurn of six years the 2/24th went to Rangoon in the autumn of 1865, but supplied three officers and 100 men for duty on the Andaman Islands. In May 1867, when the crew of a British ship were reported to have been murdered by natives of the Little Andamans, a party of the 2/24th was sent to investigate. Arriving at the scene of the reputed massacre, the troops manned two boats and rowed inshore. Only one boat's crew managed to get ashore through the heavy surf and immediately started to search for evidence, while the second boat rowed along to cover their movements. As the small party advanced, they were attacked by natives, who forced the soldiers to take cover behind a rock, where they found the skull of a European. Their ammunition nearly exhausted, they made a dash for their boat which unfortunately capsized as they tried to embark. So they made their way to the original landing-place, on the way discovering the bodies of four more Europeans.

The situation was now desperate and volunteers were called for to sail a gig inshore and pick up the stranded men. Assistant Surgeon Douglas and Privates Bell, Cooper, Griffiths, and Murphy undertook the mission and, although in constant danger of overturning, managed to save the whole shore party. The brave conduct of these men was recognized when they became the first members of the regiment to be awarded the Victoria Cross.

In 1868 the 2/24th transferred to India, eventually returning to England in 1873, whence they joined the 1/24th in South Africa in 1878.

At the time of the 2/24th's arrival the 1st

Battalion had already been on active service for three years, campaigning against the Kaffirs in the Transkei. Having subdued the Kaffir rebellion, the reasonably confident troops were to be faced with a far stronger and better organized enemy, the Zulus, perhaps the finest close-combat fighters in the world.

Other ranks' shako-plate, 1869–79. The officer's pattern was similar, but had the addition of a silver Sphinx on a tablet inscribed 'Egypt', below the Garter belt. (Author's collection)

The Zulu War

In April 1877 Sir Henry Bartle Edward Frere was appointed Governor of Cape Colony. Frere, a long and distinguished career in the Indian Service behind him, was confident that he could solve the problems of Southern Africa. He was sure that the antagonism between Briton and Boer could be checked and that the only real obstacle to confederation was the autonomous Zulu nation ruled by King Cetewayo. In Frere's opinion it was imperative that this 'irresponsible, bloodthirsty and treacherous despot' should be crushed and so 'relieve South Africa of the Zulu incubus'.

By annexing the Transvaal the British inherited the boundary dispute between the Boers and the Zulus. Frere offered to set up a commission to study the problem, hoping that they would find in favour of the Boers, thus limiting Zulu power. To his surprise the report he received awarded the disputed territory to the Zulus. On 11 December 1878 the findings were imparted to Cetewayo's envoys, but coupled with it was an ultimatum which demanded that the Zulu army should be disbanded, that the King's celibate warriors should be allowed to marry, and that the King should make compensation for certain outrages and hand over the men responsible. A clash was inevitable, for compliance would have ended Zulu independence once and for all. When the thirty days' grace expired British troops marched into Zululand, an invasion that would surely have been stopped had London been informed of it.

The Commander-in-Chief of Her Majesty's Forces in South Africa, Frederic Augustus

Thesiger, 2nd Baron Chelmsford, had decided on his plan of campaign. Three columns would enter Zululand from different points and converge on Cetewayo's capital at Ulundi. On 11 January 1879 Chelmsford and his staff crossed the Buffalo River at Rorke's Drift, the central column being commanded by Colonel Glyn, late of the 24th. This, the strongest column, consisted of seven companies of the 1/24th, eight companies of the 2/24th, two squadrons of Mounted Infantry, two battalions of the Natal Native Contingent, 200 Natal Volunteers, and 150 Mounted Police, supported by six guns and two rocket tubes of the Royal Artillery and a half-company of Royal Engineers. 'B' Company, 2/24th under Lieutenant Gonville Bromhead, were left at the Drift to guard the stores and hospital

Hampered by the weather and rough terrain, it took the column ten days to cover the first eight miles. On the 20th, a general advance was made to the new camp site at Mount Isandhlwana, a

The 24th at Isandhlwana, 22 January 1879; a painting by
Charles E. Fripp. (National Army Museum)

large outcrop of rock that the men of the 24th
thought bore a strange resemblance to their
Sphinx badge. The camp was situated on the
eastern side of Isandhlwana which slopes gently
down to a deep gully, running almost parallel to
the mountain.

During the afternoon of 21 January Major
Dartnell of the Natal Native Contingent (N.N.C.),
who had been sent out with a small force to recon-
noitre the foothills to the south-east, came across
several hundred Zulus. Thinking that they might
be part of the main impi, Dartnell requested
reinforcements so that he could attack the next
morning. At about 4 a.m. Chelmsford, accompanied by Colonel Glyn with four guns and six
companies of the 2/24th, headed south-east, leaving headquarters and five companies of the 1/24th
under Lieutenant-Colonel Pulleine and 'G' Company 2/24th with the colours of that Battalion.
The 1st Battalion had their Queen's colour in the
camp, the regimental colour having been left at

Helpmakaar. Before departing, Chelmsford
ordered Colonel Anthony Durnford R.E. to
advance with his reserve column from Rorke's
Drift and reinforce Pulleine.

At about 8 a.m. a report reached Pulleine that
a Zulu impi was approaching the camp from the
north-east. He immediately put the camp under
arms and sent a dispatch to Chelmsford. No Zulus
were seen until about 9 a.m., when a small
number were spotted on the distant hills; but
they soon moved out of sight to the north-west.

At 10 a.m. Durnford arrived in camp and,
hearing that the Zulus were in the vicinity,
decided to ride out across the plain and take
offensive action when he found them. To support
him, Pulleine ordered 'A' Company (Lieutenant
C. W. Cavaye) to take up position on a ridge
about 1,500 yards to the north. At about midday
heavy firing was heard from the north-east.
Captain George Shepstone, Durnford's staff
officer, had encountered some 20,000 Zulus who

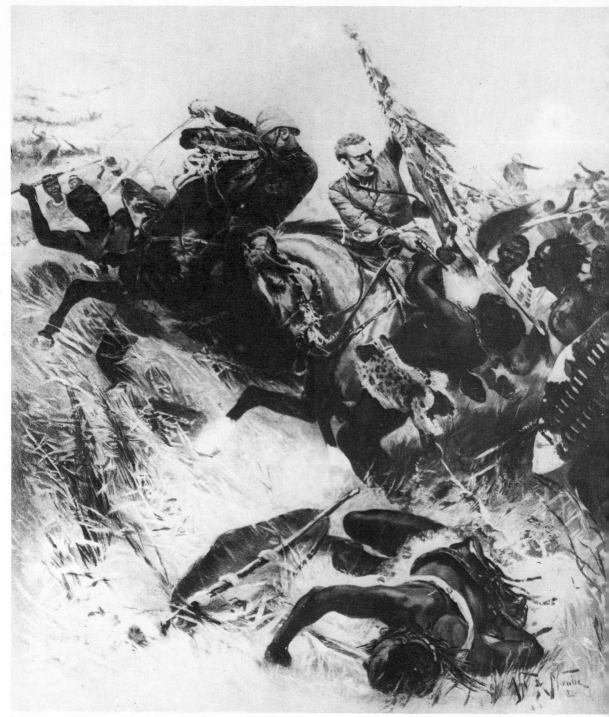

Lieutenants Melvill and Coghill saving the Queen's colour at
Isandhlwana, 22 January 1879; from a painting by Alphonse
de Neuville. (Author's collection)

were advancing on the camp. Sending a rider to
warn Durnford of the danger, Shepstone galloped
back to Pulleine to ask for reinforcements, as his
small force was slowly being driven back.

Pulleine reluctantly sent 'F' Company (Captain
W. E. Mostyn) to reinforce Cavaye on the ridge
he then sent another dispatch to Chelmsford and
had the buglers sound the 'Stand to'.

On the ridge, 'A' and 'F' Companies were now heavily engaged with the enemy, pouring volley after volley into a horde of advancing Zulus. The two companies were ordered to fall back nearer the camp, where they were joined by 'C' Company (Captain R. Younghusband).

On the plain Durnford received Shepstone's message, but it came a little too late, for a few minutes afterwards a mass of Zulus appeared and charged towards him. Firing as they went, Durnford's men retreated to the wide gully in front of the camp where they halted and took up a defensive position.

The British perimeter was made up as follows: to the left of the camp and facing north, 'A', 'F', and 'C' Companies; on their right, at an angle between them and the front-line defences, the Natal Native Contingent. All these companies were in extended order. On the extreme left of the front line were two artillery pieces with, to their right, two companies of the 1/24th and Lieutenant Pope's Company ('G') of the 2/24th, all in extended order but with large gaps between them. Durnford's men, having been forced to quit the gully, were to the right, where they were making their last gallant stand.

The soldiers of the 24th kept up a heavy and sustained fire against the advancing Zulus, so effectively that at one point the attack was checked – but only for a brief moment. The defenders were running short of ammunition, for the boxes, containing some 480,000 rounds, were tightly fastened and only a few could be opened. As the fire slackened along the front line the Zulus charged. The Natal Native Contingent, panic-stricken, fled, leaving a large opening through which Cetewayo's 'celibate, man-destroying gladiators' charged, outflanking the infantry on either side. Cavaye's and Mostyn's Companies were hacked to pieces before they even had time to fix bayonets. Pope's 'G' Company of the 2/24th with 'E' and 'H' Companies of the 1/24th lasted a little longer, but a charge by the Zulus overwhelmed 'E' Company and pushed 'H' Company towards the tents where they too were wiped out. Most of Pope's Company fell in small groups as they fought their way back towards the *nek*, but the remainder, still led by Pope, kept firing and lunging with their bayonets

The Defence of Rorke's Drift; from a painting by Alphonse de Neuville. (Parker Gallery)

until the overwhelming black mass cut them down where they stood. Among those killed in 'G' Company, 2/24th, was Private Griffiths, one of the men awarded the V.C. for gallantry at the Andaman Islands. Younghusband's Company succeeded in falling back to the southern slopes of the mountain where after a bitter struggle they were surrounded and killed to a man.

By 2 p.m. it was all over. As the Zulus moved round the camp disembowelling the dead British soldiers and killing their own badly wounded comrades, the small number of survivors were struggling to reach safety in the direction of Rorke's Drift. Forced by the Zulus to change direction, the fugitives started to make their way to the Buffalo River where most of those who reached the bank were killed by the pursuing warriors. Of the almost 1,800 men in the camp at Isandhlwana only fifty-five Europeans and perhaps 300 Natal Kaffirs managed to escape.

A short time after the Zulus had broken through the line Lieutenant-Colonel Pulleine gave the Queen's colour of the 1/24th to Lieutenant Teignmouth Melvill, the Adjutant, and ordered him to carry the honour of the regiment to safety. As Melvill wheeled his horse and made for the Buffalo River, Pulleine returned to his tent, where he was killed a short time afterwards.

After cutting his way out of the camp Melvill was joined by Lieutenant Nevill Coghill, Colonel Glyn's orderly officer, who had injured his knee and had therefore been left in the camp that morning. The two men rode to the river together, plunged their horses into the raging torrent, and made for the other side. Coghill got across safely, but Melvill, hampered by the colour, was washed off his horse and swept downstream. Seeing his brother officer in difficulty, Coghill turned back into the river to help him. A large party of Zulus had now reached the bank and those with rifles were firing at the two men. One of the bullets killed Coghill's horse, plunging its rider into the swiftly flowing river. Eventually both men reached the bank, but unfortunately Melvill had lost his grip on the colour and it floated off downstream. After clambering up a steep slope that led away from the river the two officers were finally overtaken and killed.

Melvill and Coghill were buried where they fell, at the top of what is still called Fugitives' Drift, and in 1907 were posthumously awarded the Victoria Cross. The colour was found by a patrol on 4 February a quarter of a mile downstream. The 2nd Battalion colours were lost during the battle.

Lord Chelmsford received Pulleine's message at 9.30 a.m., but as no sign of the Zulus could be seen near the camp from his position he felt no cause for concern, although he did send Commandant Brown's battalion of Native Contingent to ensure his lines of communication. When he reached the new camp site, several officers told Chelmsford that a large number of Zulus could be seen in the vicinity of Isandhlwana. Eventually he received a message from Brown: 'For God's sake come back: the camp is surrounded.' At 2 p.m. he started back towards Isandhlwana. Five miles from the camp an exhausted Commandant Lonsdale, an officer in Major Dartnell's Native Contingent, approached them with the news that the camp had been captured. That night Chelmsford's weary troops bivouacked among their dead comrades on the battlefield. All was quiet, but in the distance they heard the sounds of another battle coming from the direction of Rorke's Drift, where 'B' Company, 2/24th, under Lieutenant Gonville Bromhead had been left as a permanent garrison.

The morning of 22 January had been quiet at Rorke's Drift, the Swedish Mission Station commandeered by the army for use as a hospital and commissariat store. Situated on the Natal side of the Buffalo River, it consisted of two buildings some thirty yards apart, a mud-brick thatched house being used as a hospital and a barn serving as a storeroom. The river lay some 800 yards below the post; behind, at a distance of 400 yards, was a large, rocky hill which the Swedish missionary, Otto Witt, had named the Oskarberg.

At about 2 p.m. Major Spalding, the commander of the post, rode to Helpmakaar, for he was anxious to find out why a company of the 1/24th, which was to augment the garrison, was two days overdue. In his absence the command devolved on Lieutenant John R. M. Chard, R.E.

At 3.15 p.m., as Chard was checking the *pont* down by the river, two mounted figures galloped into sight and splashed across the drift. Lieutenant

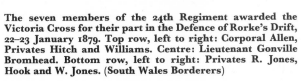

The seven members of the 24th Regiment awarded the
Victoria Cross for their part in the Defence of Rorke's Drift,
22–23 January 1879. Top row, left to right: Corporal Allen,
Privates Hitch and Williams. Centre: Lieutenant Gonville
Bromhead. Bottom row, left to right: Privates R. Jones,
Hook and W. Jones. (South Wales Borderers)

Adendorff and Vane of the Natal Native Contingent reported the disastrous encounter at Isandhlwana and went on to say that a Zulu impi was now advancing on Rorke's Drift. Adendorff said he would stay to help in the defence of the station while Vane galloped off to warn the garrison at Helpmakaar.

Chard returned to the post to find that Lieutenant Bromhead had also received the news, as well as orders to strengthen the station. The two officers, assisted by J. L. Dalton of the Army Commissariat Department, immediately set about barricading the windows in the hospital and storeroom, piercing loopholes in the walls and constructing a breastwork four feet high connecting the two buildings. A cross-wall, joining the storeroom with the northern breastwork, was also built as a second line of defence. Fortunately the necessary materials were at hand in the form of two wagons, bags of mealies, and biscuit boxes.

The total force that Chard could call upon was eighty-four men of Bromhead's 'B' Company, a few casuals from other regiments, and about 300 men of the Natal Native Contingent, a total of about 400 men, excluding the hospital patients.

While the work was in progress, Chard rode down to the river to make sure that the ponts had been secured in midstream and to order the men back to the post. Sergeant Milne of the Buffs, along with the civilian pont-man, Daniells, volunteered to moor the ponts in midstream and defend them from their decks with a few men. Chard refused, as he could ill afford the men, and then started back.

As he approached the station, at about 3.30 p.m. an officer of Durnford's Horse with his troop arrived and asked for instructions. Chard requested him to cover the ponts and to send out patrols in the direction from which the enemy were expected. As the impi advanced, they were to fall back on the post and assist in its defence. At about 4.15 p.m. after firing a few shots, the men of Durnford's Horse and their officer fled in the direction of Helpmakaar. At the same time the detachment of the N.N.C. also deserted the post, reducing the total force to some 139 men, of whom only 104 were fit for duty. As the perimeter was now too large for the few men left to defend, Chard ordered the retrenchment of the wall, but even as the work was begun the first Zulus appeared from behind the Oskarberg Hill and charged at the southern wall.

At 500 yards the men of the 24th opened a sustained fire and managed to keep the Zulus at a distance, but, taking advantage of the broken ground and uncut bush, the warriors eventually managed to reach the outer defences. From the slopes of the Oskarberg Hill the few Zulus who had rifles sniped down on to the soldiers who were now engaged in a hand-to-hand struggle. At the northern wall the Zulus were actually reaching up and trying to pull the bayonets off the rifles. Time and again the Zulus would charge the perimeter, concentrating their attacks on the hospital and the front barricade. On being repulsed they would take cover wherever they could and then, with a total disregard for their lives, would rush forward once more.

Chard was soon forced to withdraw his men to the second line of defence, a wall of biscuit boxes that bisected the original perimeter, leaving the hospital in a desperate situation. A number of

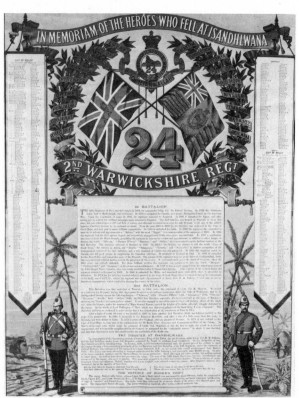

Memorial Roll to the officers and men of the 24th killed at Isandhlwana. (National Army Museum)

1 Private, 1742
2 Grenadier, 1751
3 Grenadier, 1768

1 **Sergeant, Grenadier Company, 1808**
2 **Officer, 1808**
3 **Officer, 1790**

B

MICHAEL ROF

1 Private, 1813
2 Officer, levee dress, 1822
3 Officer, 1832

CHAEL ROFFE

C

1 Corporal, 1840
2 Pioneer, 1849
3 Officer, 1855

MICHAEL ROF

1 Officer, 1865
2 Private, 1879
3 Officer, undress uniform, 1894

MICHAEL ROFFE

E

1 Sergeant, 1895
2 Private, 1900
3 Officer, mess dress, 1895

MICHAEL ROFFE

1 Battalion Intelligence Officer, 1915
2 Private, 4th Battalion, S.W.B., 1916
3 Drum-Major, full dress, 1928

MICHAEL ROFFE

1 R.S.M., 1936
2 Officer, 1942
3 Officer, Royal Regiment of Wales, 1970

MICHAEL ROFF

Lieutenant-Colonel J. M. G. Tongue (left) with Lieutenants Phipps and Weallens, the colour party and colours, after Queen Victoria had decorated the recovered Queen's colour with a wreath of immortelles. Note that the colour-sergeants and private are wearing the 1869–78 shako-plate on the helmet. (Author's collection)

patients had already left to fight at the barricades, while those who remained and could fire a rifle were doing their best to help the soldiers detailed for the building's defence.

At 6 p.m., having failed to break into the hospital, the Zulus managed to set fire to the thatched roof, forcing the immediate evacuation of the patients. Hampered by the lack of inter-communicating doors, the handful of soldiers hacked through the inner walls and passed the sick from room to room, keeping the enemy at bay as they went. In the last room Privates Hook, Williams, R. Jones, and W. Jones started to lift the eleven patients through a small window from which they were to run, crawl, or be carried across an open piece of ground towards the store-house defences. Nine of the eleven made it. Of the two who died, one was assegaied as he crossed the gap and the other, Sergeant Maxfield, was delirious and refused to leave his bed and was eventually stabbed to death by the Zulus.

While the fire continued to burn, the battle raged on. Two of the walking wounded, Corporal Allen and Private Hitch, although unable to use their rifles, made themselves useful by supplying their hard-pressed comrades with ammunition. At 4 a.m. the hospital fire flickered and died and

with it the Zulu attacks. At sunrise the only Zulus in sight were the 350 or so who lay dead round the perimeter. The losses of the garrison were seventeen killed or died of wounds and ten wounded.

Of the eleven Victoria Crosses granted for the defence, seven of them went to men of the 24th, Lieutenant Gonville Bromhead, Corporal Allen, and Privates Hitch, Hook, R. Jones, W. Jones, and Williams, the greatest number of V.C.s ever awarded to one regiment in one action.

The might of the Zulu Empire was finally smashed at the Battle of Ulundi in July 1879 and with the capture of King Cetewayo the following month.

In 1880 the regiment having returned from South Africa, the Queen expressed a wish to see the colour rescued by Melvill and Coghill. On 28 July Lieutenant-Colonel J. M. G. Tongue, with Lieutenants Phipps and Weallens and an escort of four colour-sergeants, took the colours to Osborne, where Queen Victoria attached a wreath of immortelles to the pole of the Queen's colour, 'To commemorate the devoted gallantry of Lieutenant and Adjutant T. Melvill and Lieutenant N. J. A. Coghill . . . and in recognition of the noble defence of Rorke's Drift'.

A New Title

As far back as 1877 a committee under Colonel Stanley had recommended that line and militia battalions should be more closely connected and furthermore, 'we consider this is best to be effected by their being treated as one regiment, such regiment wearing a Territorial designation; the Line Battalions being the 1st and 2nd; the Militia Battalions the 3rd and 4th etc, of such Territorial regiment; the Depot being common to all, and being the last battalion of the series.' In February 1881 the Ellice Committee put forward certain proposals on the formation of Territorial regiments. On 1 July 1881 the 24th changed their title of '2nd Warwickshire' for that of the 'South Wales Borderers'. This change of title was not as keenly felt as in some other regiments, as for the

Other ranks' helmet-plate, 1881–1901. (Author's collection)

remained there until October 1892, when they changed stations for Aden. The following October the battalion embarked for England. In December 1892 the 1/24th went on foreign service to Egypt then to Gibraltar and finally to India in 1897.

On the outbreak of the South African War, 11 October 1899, the 2nd Battalion, having just moved to Ireland, was not included in the army corps dispatched to the Cape. Only after the reverses at Magersfontein, Colenso, and Stormberg, referred to as 'Black Week', were they sent out, landing at Cape Town on 3 February 1900 as part of the 15th Brigade in the 7th Division.

In February and March 1900 the battalion took part in Lord Roberts's operations for the relief of Kimberley, coming under fire for the first time at Jacobsdal on 15 February, when the 15th Brigade attacked in force and drove some 300 Boers from their positions. At Cronje's surrender at Paardeberg, 27 February, the battalion was represented by its mounted infantry companies, the remainder of the 2nd not being committed.

On 8 March 1900 the 3rd (Militia) Battalion of the regiment landed at the Cape *en route* for Kimberley where it did great service in guarding the communications on Lord Roberts's left flank. After the capture of Pretoria and the general dispersion of the Boers the struggle developed into guerrilla warfare with sharp isolated actions, long marches, but no sustained fighting. This situation lasted until 31 May 1902, when the Boers signed the Peace Treaty at Vereeniging.

past eight years their depot had been at Brecon and their recruiting done along the Welsh border. The change which probably saddened the regiment was the loss of their green facings for white, as the reforms made no distinction between English and Welsh non-Royal regiments. Another blow was the official loss of the cherished numeral '24', although unofficially the South Wales Borderers continued to be known as the '24th'.

While the 1/24th were stationed in England, the 2nd Battalion left South Africa for Gibraltar where, on 6 August 1880, they were presented with new colours by Lord Napier of Magdala. Two years later they quitted the Rock and sailed for India. The year 1886 saw the battalion once more on active service, this time in Burma, where they helped to suppress King Theebaw's rebellion. The two and a half years spent in Burma cost the 2/24th some sixty casualties, mostly from disease. In November 1888 they returned to India and

Officers of the 24th in Egypt, 1895. (South Wales Borderers)

Single lock bridge constructed in little over an hour by 'D' Company, 2nd Battalion, South Wales Borderers at Aldershot, 1897. Note that the men are wearing the field cap which replaced the glengarry. (South Wales Borderers)

he casualties sustained by the 2/24th during the ar amounted to 216 men, ninety-five of them om disease.

The 2nd Battalion remained on garrison duty in outh Africa until May 1904, when they sailed for ngland. One year later the regiment was granted ermission to resume the cherished green facings lat they had lost in 1881. In 1912 the battalion as posted to Tientsin, where they were included a the international force which had been uartered in North China since the Boxer ebellion of 1900.

The 1/24th returned to England in 1910 after foreign tour of eighteen years in which they had en no active service. As part of the 3rd Brigade in le 1st Division they were training at Borden hen assassination of Archduke Francis Ferdinand f Austria sparked off an uncontrollable chain of vents culminating in the First World War of 914–18.

The World Wars

At the outbreak of the war the 1st Battalion went to France as part of Britain's 'contemptible little army'. Within three weeks of mobilization they were in action at Mons, then for thirteen days they endured the hardships of the Great Retreat, although in both of these they hardly saw any real action. When Joffre staged a counter-attack the B.E.F. advanced with him and drove the Germans back across the Marne and came to grips with them on the northern heights of the Aisne. The battalion lost eight officers and 200 men during the German counter-attack on Mont Faucon, and received the personal congratulations of Sir Douglas Haig: 'The conduct of the South Wales Borderers in driving back the strong attack made on them is particularly deserving of praise.'

In October 1914 the battalion was transferred to Flanders where they came in for some very tough fighting at Ypres. On 31 October the German attacks strengthened and carried Gheluvelt, seeming to break the British line. The 1/24th were in the grounds of Château Gheluvelt and with 'indomitable courage and dogged tenacity' managed to hold their position until reinforced by the 2nd Worcesters, who counter-attacked and drove the Germans back, thereby securing the flank. For the Worcesters and the 24th Gheluvelt ranks as one of the great days in their histories and is remembered with special pride. If the 24th had not held their position, the Worcesters' counter-attack would have been impossible, and had the advance failed the efforts of the 24th would have been useless.

For the remainder of the war the battalion fought with the 1st Division on the Somme in 1916,

Officers of the Regiment at Karachi, 1908. (South Wales Borderers)

at Ypres in 1917, and in the breaking of the Hindenburg Line in 1918. After the signing of the Armistice they marched with the rest of the division into Germany as part of the Army of Occupation.

The 2nd Battalion had nearly completed two years' service in North China when war broke out. In August 1914 the Japanese entered the conflict against the Germans and the 2/24th, along with the 36th Sikhs, joined them for the capture of the German base of Tsingtao. At 6.30 a.m. on 7 November Tsingtao fell at a cost to the battalion of fourteen men killed or died of wounds or disease and two officers and thirty-four men wounded. The battle honour 'Tsingtao', is held by no other British regiment.

In January 1915 the 2/24th returned to England and joined the 87th Brigade of the 29th Division. Their stay at home was a short one, for in March they left England for the attack on the Gallipoli Peninsula, where, on 25 April 1915, the 29th Division made its famous landing at Helles. At 'S' Beach in particular the men of the 2nd Battalion proved their worth. Three companies covered by the guns of H.M.S. *Cornwallis*, made an efficient landing and dislodged the Turks from their defensive position for the comparatively light cost of two officers and eighteen men killed and drowned and two officers and forty men wounded. The 2/24th served throughout the rest of the Gallipoli campaign and took part in the final evacuation of the peninsula on 8 January 1916.

Second Lieutenant Morgan-Owen (seated, left) in the Transvaal, 1900. He was appointed Colonel of the Regiment in 1931. Note the differences in dress between the mounted infantryman (standing, right) and the infantryman (centre). (South Wales Borderers)

In March 1916 the 29th Division arrived in France, where they remained for the rest of the war, taking part in the actions at Beaumont Hamel and Cambrai and helping to check the German offensive on the Lys in April 1918. At the end of the war they formed part of the Army of Occupation in Cologne.

The Territorial and Service units of the South Wales Borderers, between them, raised sixteen battalions and saw active service in France, Gallipoli, Mesopotamia, and Macedonia. It was the 10th (1st Gwent) Battalion that furnished one of the regiment's heroes, C.S.M. Jack Williams, who finished the war with the V.C., D.C.M., M.M. and Bar, and the Medaille Militaire, one of the most decorated soldiers of the First World War.

During this 'war to end all wars' the 24th won six Victoria Crosses as well as numerous other decorations, seventy-four battle honours, ten of which are borne on the Queen's colour, for the loss of no fewer than 5,777 officers and other ranks.

A private with the regimental mascots (wildebeestes) at Tidworth, 1905. (South Wales Borderers)

Bandsman and band-boys, 1907. (South Wales Borderers)

Private in review order, c. 1910.
(South Wales Borderers)

Drummer, c. 1910.
(National Army Museum)

Between the Wars

The First World War had ended, but the years between 1919 and 1939 were not particularly peaceful for the 1st and 2nd Battalions, who were employed on internal security duties in the major trouble-spots of the Empire. The 1st Battalion was in Ireland during the 'Troubles' of 1920–2, and in 1928 moved to Cairo whence, after less than a year, they were sent to the mandated territories of Palestine. They returned to Egypt in 1929 and in October of the following year sailed for Hong Kong, where they were to spend four years, during which time they were presented with new colours to replace the famous Isandhlwana set. In 1934 the battalion landed in India, where they helped to put down the various tribal revolts that occurred along the North-West Frontier.

The 2nd Battalion was stationed in India between 1919 and 1927, when they moved to Aden for a year before returning to England. In 1935 the battalion was sent to strengthen the garrison at Malta when a state of tension had developed between England and Italy over Mussolini's threat to Abyssinia. In mid-1936, after the occupation of Addis Ababa by Italian troops, the situation altered and the 2nd Battalion was moved to Palestine, where the Arabs were once more in open conflict with the Jews.

For the first two years of the Second World War the 1st Battalion remained in India, but in 1941, in response to the threat of a German attack on the oilfields of Iraq, it was moved to Qaiyara and then to Mosul. In May 1942, as part of the 20th Indian Brigade of the 10th Indian Division, the battalion was ordered to Egypt, where Rommel's offensive was in full swing.

With the other members of their brigade the battalion formed a defensive 'box' at Bel Hamed near Tobruk, which was still holding out. This box was ordered to be defended to the last, but on 17 June orders were received to withdraw to Sollum, some seventy miles east. To try to outwit the enemy who lay across the route in great strength, the commanding officer decided to drive the convoy south and then east in a bid to outflank them. During the journey many of the vehicles were either lost or hit and only a few managed to reach their objective. Of the battalion who had left Bel Hamed only four officers and about one hundred men got through safely, the rest, some 500 men of all ranks, were taken prisoner.

The withdrawal continued through El Alamein, where the Germans were eventually halted, to Cairo where the remnants of the battalion were augmented by a draft of fifteen officers and 300 men, prior to their embarkation for Cyprus. In mid-August, while they were awaiting reinforcements, the battalion was ordered to disband. This order came as a great shock to the men who were mostly transferred to the 1st King's Own Royal Regiment, while a small cadre joined the 4th Battalion Monmouthshire Regiment in England. In December 1942 the 4th Monmouths became the 1st Battalion South Wales Borderers.

When the Germans invaded Norway and Denmark in 1940, the 2nd Battalion became part of a small Allied force, which included Polish and French troops, sent to help the Norwegian Army. In April the battalion landed at Harstad, boarded some Norwegian fishing-boats, and moved to the Andenes Peninsula, where they were to support a French push towards Narvik. They advanced along the peninsula until orders for their withdrawal were received. At Harstad they embarked on the cruiser *Effingham* which sailed

Other ranks of the 2nd South Wales Borderers at the British Barracks at Tientsin, 1914. (South Wales Borderers)

Guard of Honour of the 2nd South Wales Borderers at Tientsin, 12 June 1914. (National Army Museum)

for the West Fiord. The next day the cruiser struck an uncharted rock and had to be abandoned, the men on board transferring to an escorting destroyer and continuing their journey. For the rest of the campaign the battalion defended Bodö, where an airfield was under construction. After the invasion of Belgium and Holland and the disastrous events in France, the whole Allied force in Norway was evacuated. In this small campaign the 2nd Battalion lost thirteen men wounded and six killed.

The 2/24th were the only Welsh battalion to take part in the Normandy landings of 6 June 1944. They landed at Le Hamel at midday, captured the bridge at Vaux-sur-Aisne, and by the end of the day had covered more ground than any other battalion in the assault.

For the next eleven months they fought through France (Sully, Caen, Falaise, Risle Crossing, Le Havre), Belgium (Antwerp–Turnhout Canal) and Holland (Zetten, Arnhem), ending up in Hamburg in May 1945.

In 1940, in view of the threat of a German invasion of England, three new battalions were raised, the 5th, 6th, and 7th South Wales Borderers. The 5th was a home defence unit until their disbandment in 1943. The 6th became a tank unit, the 158th Regiment, Royal Armoured Corps (South Wales Borderers), until in 1943 it was reconverted to infantry and sent to Burma, where it did sterling service against the Japanese (Burma 1944–5, Mayu Tunnels, Sahmaw Chaung, Pinwe, the Shweli, Myitson). The 7th Battalion was eventually transferred to the Royal Artillery. The 2nd and 3rd Battalions of the Monmouthshire Regiment fought in North-west Europe from shortly after 'D' Day until the end of the war, when the 2nd passed into suspended animation and the 3rd was disbanded. The 1st (Rifle) Battalion the Monmouthshire Regiment had transferred to the Royal Artillery (T.A.) in 1938 and therefore ceased to belong to the corps of the South Wales Borderers.

The 2nd Worcesters passing through the 1st South Wales
Borderers at Château Gheluvelt, 31 October 1914. (South
Wales Borderers)

An End
and a Beginning

The years immediately after the Second World
War saw the birth of the brigade system and the
rapid reduction of the army. On 31 May 1948 the
regiment's 2nd Battalion was formally disbanded,
the majority of the men being transferred to other
regiments in the Welsh Brigade.

In October 1945 the 1st Battalion sailed from
Southampton for Palestine, but after only seven
months they moved to Cyprus to guard the
thousands of Jews who had been detained while
trying to enter Palestine illegally. In 1949, when
Britain recognized the State of Israel and gave up
her mandate, the battalion moved to the Sudan,
where two companies were detached to the Red
Sea hills, while the remainder of the unit stayed at
Khartoum. Hardly a week had passed when a

tactical headquarters and one company were
dispatched to Asmara, in the ex-Italian colony of
Eritrea, to help the 1st Battalion Royal Berkshire
Regiment in operations against a group of bandits
called *shifta*. When Eritrea was united with
Ethiopia the 1/24th returned to Wales, but only
for a short stay, for in January 1953 they moved to
Germany, where they remained for nearly two
years.

In September 1955 the battalion sailed from
Southampton for Malaya for active service
against the Communist terrorists who were
waging a guerrilla war. Landing at Singapore on
19 October, the regiment took over the camp at
Kluang from the 1st East Yorkshire Regiment.
Their job consisted in flushing out and destroying
the isolated pockets of Communist rebels, a task
which they performed well, for within a few
months one of the leading terrorists, Kok Fui, had
been killed. In 1956 the battalion moved to
Segamat, in the State of Johore, where they
destroyed the Selumpur branch of the rebels, an
action which was followed by the surrender of
their leader, Ming Lee. In April 1958, having

Colour party at the Citadel, Cairo, 1929. (South Wales Borderers)

changes had occurred in the armed forces: loss of regimental depots, widespread amalgamations, and the adoption of brigade badges. The Welsh Brigade badge consisted of upright Prince of Wales's Feathers with the motto, '*Ich Dien*'.

In the summer of 1959 the battalion once more moved to Germany as part of the 11th Infantry Group based at Minden. Three years later they flew to Hong Kong, where, as well as their normal duties, they supplied one officer and fifteen men to the United Nations Platoon which formed the Honour Guard at Seoul in South Korea.

In January 1967, after only a few months in England, the regiment was posted to Aden, where in their nine-month tour they were engaged in some 300 terrorist actions in which they killed and wounded twenty-two terrorists and captured eighteen, for the loss of two men killed and thirty-three wounded.

In the White Paper published by Mr Wilson's Government in July 1967, drastic cuts in the armed forces were proposed. The Welsh Brigade was to reduce by one battalion, the 1st Welch Regiment, and to amalgamate with the South Wales Borderers to form a new regiment.

On 11 June 1969, in the shadow of the tower of Cardiff Castle, the South Wales Borderers and the Welch Regiment died, to be reborn as the Royal Regiment of Wales, a regiment which its Colonel-in-Chief, Prince Charles, affirmed would become 'the pride of Wales'.

spent most of their last two years' service in Malaya on internal security duties in Singapore, the battalion returned to Wales, where they became part of the 2nd Infantry Brigade in the newly formed Strategic Reserve.

During their tour of duty in the Far East many

The Plates

1 Private, 1742

The first reliable information on the uniforms of the 24th Regiment appeared in the *Clothing Book of* 1742, plate 57. This plate, part of the set engraved by John Pine by order of the Duke of Cumberland, shows a private of the regiment wearing the large broad-skirted red coat with cuffs and lapels in green. At this period the facings and skirt linings were usually of the same colour, but in the engraving the skirt linings are shown as white. The black felt tricorn hat had, in the case of the 24th, the edge taped in white.

2 Grenadier, 1751

The most outstanding feature of the grenadier's uniform at this period was undoubtedly the 'mitre' cap. The cap of the 24th had a green cloth front, 12 in. high, edged in white tape and embroidered with the royal cipher, 'G.R.', in white worsted with a crown in heraldic colours above and foliage on each side. The front flap was in red cloth, edged in white and ornamented with the white horse of Hanover and the motto, '*Nec Aspera Terrent*'. The headband at the back of the cap was in green cloth, embroidered with leaves and the regimental number in white worsted.

3 Grenadier, 1768

The *Clothing Warrant* of 1768 abolished the cloth grenadier cap and replaced it with one in black bearskin, bearing a black-japanned copper plate with the raised parts in silver plate. The red cloth coat was lapelled to the waist in green cloth and fastened by means of ten pewter buttons with buttonholes taped in regimental-pattern tape, white worsted with a red and green line.

B1 Sergeant, Grenadier Company, 1808

The short coat, introduced in 1796, was of red cloth with green facings and fastened down the front with eight buttons set in pairs. All sergeants' tape was plain white and not of regimental pattern. A General Order dated July 1802 distinguished sergeant-majors by four chevrons in silver lace, sergeants by three chevrons in white tape, and corporals by two chevrons in tape of regimental pattern. The sergeant's waist-sash was crimson with a central stripe of regimental colour. A Horse Guards circular of 20 October 1806 abolished the lacquered shako introduced in 1800 and replaced it with one in felt which tapered slightly to the top. The plate worn on the previous pattern was retained, i.e. approximately 6 in. by 4 in., bearing the Garter with the motto '*Honi soit qui mal y pense*', with the royal cipher in the centre surmounted by a crown, with a trophy of arms and flags behind and a lion beneath.

B2 Officer, 1808

Although the men's cocked hat had been discontinued by the General Order of 24 February 1800, officers still continued with it, wearing it fore and aft and ornamented with a red and white plume. The lapels of the coat were often worn with the tops turned back, revealing the green

1st Battalion colours and silver drums, 1930. The Queen's colour (left) is that saved by Lieutenants Melvill and Coghill at Isandhlwana. These colours were in use until 1 April 1934, when they were laid up at Brecon. (South Wales Borderers)

facing and silver lace button-loops. In about 1802 a new crossbelt plate had been adopted. Oval in shape, it was engraved with a Garter belt surmounted by a crown, with the title 'Warwickshire Regt' on the belt and the number '24' in the centre. Surrounding the belt was a laurel wreath. Below the Garter was the Sphinx over 'Egypt' and on either side of the crown the royal cipher, 'G' on the left and 'R' on the right.

B3 Officer, 1790

By 1790 the tricorn hat had the sides and back turned up much higher, so high in fact that they had to be laced up in position. The coat had green facings and white turnbacks, though the latter was now universal and not a regimental distinction. The cuffs were small and round, measuring $3\frac{1}{2}$ in. deep and ornamented with button-loops and buttons. The white baldrick and crossbelt plate were introduced in about 1788. The plate was in silver with a matted surface with a beaded border, and in the centre an engraved star with the Garter belt and numeral 'XXIV' mounted in gilt.

C1 Private, 1813

The uniform worn at this period was the same as for 1800, except that grey overall trousers and another new shako had been introduced. Known as the 'Waterloo', 'Wellington', or 'Belgic' shako, it was authorized by a General Order of 24 February 1811. The body of the shako was of black felt for other ranks and black beaver for officers, and was cylindrical in shape, was bound round

Officers of the Regiment on the North-West Frontier, India, 1937. (South Wales Borderers)

the lower edge with black tape, and had a hig false front, also edged in tape. The front measure $8\frac{1}{2}$ in. in height, whereas the back and side measured only $6\frac{1}{2}$ in. Twisted white worsted cord were attached to the shako at each side and hun down in front above the black leather peak. Th shako-plate was roughly oval in shape, surmounte by a crown, with the royal cipher, 'GR', in th centre. A Horse Guards circular of 14 Februar 1812 permitted the use of badges and numbers o the shako-plate, but it is not known whether th 24th took advantage of this.

C2 Officer, levee dress, 1822

The 'Regency' pattern of the shako was authorize on 22 August 1815, and was a much more cumber some affair than the Waterloo shako, measurin $7\frac{1}{2}$ in. in height, with a top 11 in. in diameter. Th coat had broad green lapels, heavily ornamente with silver lace and a 'Prussian' collar, and tw pairs of silver lace button-loops and silver buttons So much lace had been introduced that th authorities issued special orders to inspectin officers to report any deviations from dres regulations. The officer who inspected the 24t Regiment on 23 October 1828 handed in th following: 'The major-general has to report that previous to March last, light blue trousers, wit silver lace, costing four pounds, and a silver waist belt, costing one pound fifteen shillings, wer introduced for dress by Lieutenant-Colone Fleming, but the only deviation from the regula tion which now exist are having badges placed or the breastplate, costing eighteen shillings, and a trifling alteration in the wings of the flank companies.'

C3 Officer, 1832

The shako remained basically the same as in 1822 except for some slight modifications that wer introduced in 1828, i.e. the height of the plume was reduced from 12 to 8 in. and the height of the shako from $7\frac{1}{2}$ to 6 in. By General Order 495 issued in 1830, all lace was to be gold for Regular regiments and silver for Militia.

D1 Corporal, 1840

A Horse Guards circular of 27 August 1835 replaced the plume on the shako with a ball tuft. In 1839 yet another change in the shako took

S.M. Watkins and Private A. Lovell, 1st Battalion South Wales Borderers, at the Bahe Pagoda, Burma, 1944. (South Wales Borderers)

Jungle patrol in Malaya, 1955–6. (South Wales Borderers)

place when a new plate was introduced. Made of brass and circular in shape, it bore the number '24' stamped in the centre on a lined background. Round the edge of the plate was a wreath of half oak leaves and half laurel leaves. Regimental-pattern tape had been abolished for other ranks in 1836 and been replaced by plain white tape. At the same time sergeants had been issued with a plain-fronted double-breasted coat.

D2 Pioneer, 1849

The 'Albert'-pattern shako was authorized on 4 December 1843. It had a body of black felt for other ranks, 6¾ in. high with a black lacquered leather top. Both the front peak and the smaller one at the back were also in lacquered leather. The illustration shows the shako with the white calico cover worn on tropical service. The following extract is from a letter written by Lieutenant-Colonel M. Smith after the Battle of Chilianwala: 'The men wore their dress caps in the action, and this sort of headdress is always found unsuited for hard work in battle. Many fell off and were lost in the mêlée, and it seems to be, on such occasions, the soldier's great desire to rid himself of so inconvenient an appendage.' In addition to the usual equipment, regimental pioneers wore buff aprons and carried axes, bill-hooks, and saw-backed short swords with brass hilts.

D3 Officer, 1855

On 16 January 1855 the 'Albert'-pattern shako was superseded by a new cap, sometimes referred to as the '2nd Albert'. Based on the contemporary French headdress, it was smaller and lighter than its predecessor but still retained the two peaks, the back one continuing the line of the shako, the front one being horizontal and squared at the end. The plate was in the form of an eight-pointed star, surmounted by a crown. On the centre of the star was the number '24' surrounded by a Garter belt bearing the motto, *'Honi soit qui mal y pense'*. The tail-coat was now abolished in favour of a double-breasted tunic which had lapels that could be buttoned back to reveal the facings or buttoned over. A crimson net sash was worn over the left shoulder and was held in place by a small scarlet twisted cord on the tunic. A waist-belt and sword slings replaced the crossbelt and elaborate plate.

United Nations Honour Guard, Korea, 1965. (South Wales Borderers)

E1 Officer, 1865

Authorized on 28 November 1860, this pattern of headdress is usually referred to as the 'quilted' shako, by virtue of the ribbed blue cloth which covered the cork body. A single-breasted tunic, introduced in 1856, replaced the double-breasted pattern. The cuffs were round with a slashed panel, both in the facing colour. The skirts at the back were ornamented with scarlet slashed panels, lace loops, and buttons.

E2 Private, 1879

The white foreign-service helmet was authorized for all ranks on 1 June 1877, although it had been worn previously in India and on other stations. Made of cork, it was covered in white cloth in six seams and had a zinc button, also covered in white cloth, fitted to the top. The equipment worn

at this date was the 'Valise' pattern, introduced in 1868. When on active service the helmet and white buff equipment were usually dyed with a solution of tea or coffee. The tunic was in scarlet cloth, the collar being ornamented with green collar-patches and the Sphinx badge. The cuffs had a pointed panel of green cloth edged in white tape which terminated in a crow's-foot knot at the point. The shoulder-straps were of scarlet cloth, edged in white tape and ornamented with the number '24' in *white metal*. The buttons were of the general-service pattern introduced in 1873, when regimental numbered buttons were discontinued for other ranks.

E3 Officer, undress uniform, 1894

The forage-cap was of dark blue cloth with a band of black oak-leaf-pattern lace round the headband.

he badge was in the form of a gilt laurel wreath, rmounted by a crown, with, in the centre, the elsh Dragon in silver on a black velvet ground. he patrol jacket was of universal pattern in dark ue cloth, braided round the edge in black with ack cords and loops across the front, and a black ustrian knot on each cuff. The trousers were in rk blue cloth with a scarlet welt down the tside seam of each leg.

1 Sergeant, 1895

eneral Order 40 of May 1878 introduced the me-service helmet, generally known as the lue cloth' helmet. The plate was a brass eight-ointed star surmounted by a crown. After 1881 e centre of the star was a circle bearing the title, outh Wales Borderers', and in the centre the elsh Dragon surrounded by a laurel wreath. he tunic was of scarlet cloth with white collar nd cuffs and fastened down the front with seven eneral-service buttons. A red cloth flap was worn n the left shoulder to prevent any rifle oil aining the tunic. The waist-belt was of white uff leather, fastening at the front with a brass niversal-pattern locket.

2 Private, 1900

he helmet shown is the foreign-service pattern, troduced in 1877, worn with the khaki cover and eck-protector. The tunic, of khaki cloth, had a tand-and-fall collar and plain cuffs. Trousers ere of the same material and were worn with uttees. The equipment was of the 'Slade Wallace' attern, which was introduced in 1888 and eplaced the 'Valise' equipment.

3 Officer, mess dress, 1895

he mess jacket was of scarlet cloth with the ollar and pointed cuffs of facing cloth, which in he case of the South Wales Borderers was white, he regiment having lost their green facings in the rmy Reforms of 1881. The edge of the jacket was ound all round, including the top and bottom of he collar, with gold braid. A row of gilt studs and ooks-and-eyes were down the leading edge. The waistcoat was in white cloth and was edged in old braid round the top and down the front and long the bottom to the side seams. The pockets were also edged in braid, with crow's-foot knots t the top, bottom, and ends.

G1 Battalion Intelligence Officer, 1915

This illustration shows an officer in service dress with ranking sewn on to the cuff-flaps. Bands of chevron tape and tracing braid were worn round the cuff according to rank, e.g. lieutenant, one row of chevron lace; captain, two rows of chevron lace; major, three rows of chevron lace with tracing braid between. The green cap-band and collar-tabs indicate that the officer is employed on intelligence duties.

G2 Private, 4th Battalion, S.W.B., 1916

The helmet worn was the foreign-service or 'Wolseley' pattern, which had a cork body covered in khaki drill cloth in six seams. The tunic and shorts were also in khaki drill, the former having two pockets at the waist and two on the chest. The equipment was the 1908 pattern.

G3 Drum-Major, full dress, 1928

The illustration is based on a photograph of Drum-Major Matthews of the 2nd Battalion. The home-service helmet was of the same pattern as

Recce Platoon finding a huge arms cache in Aden, 1967. (South Wales Borderers)

Birth of the Royal Regiment of Wales. Presentation by H.R.H. The Prince of Wales of new colours, Cardiff Castle, 1969. (South Wales Borderers)

worn by the sergeant in 1895 (Plate F1), except that the plate was now surmounted by a domed Tudor crown (in use from 1901 to 1952). The scarlet tunic had a green collar, edged in gold lace and ornamented by a collar badge – the Sphinx on a tablet inscribed 'Egypt'. The wing epaulettes were scarlet, edged and decorated with gold lace. The Drum-Major's sash was the ordnance-issue pattern of green cloth, edged in gold lace and

ornamented with the crown and royal cipher, in embroidery, with a silver shield and drumstick below and the title, 'South Wales Borderers', in gold embroidery underneath. The mace was of ebony, decorated with a silver top and silver chains.

H1 R.S.M., 1936

The tunic and shorts were in khaki drill cloth. The collar-badges, a Sphinx over 'Egypt' with 'S.W.B.' beneath, were in bronze, whereas the R.S.M.s rank badge was in polished brass. The Sam Browne belt was in brown leather with brass fittings and had a cross-strap passing over the right shoulder and fastening on the left side. The sword-frog was attached to the left side. The 1892 pattern infantry sword in a Sam Browne scabbard was worn.

H2 Officer, 1942

In 1938 the War Office, after six years of trials, finally approved a pattern of battledress, consisting of blouse, trousers, and gaiters. The waist-length blouse had buttoned cuffs, two patch pockets on the chest, and a fly-front fastening. The olive drab waist-belt was $2\frac{1}{4}$ in. wide and had a 'pistol case' on the left and an ammunition-pouch on the right.

H3 Officer, Royal Regiment of Wales, 1970

The service cap is of universal pattern in blue cloth with a scarlet band and welt round the crown, ornamented with the regimental badge. The badge, in silver, is the Prince of Wales's Feathers with the motto, 'Ich Dien'. The jacket and trousers are in blue barathea.